SECONDARY EDUCATION
IN THE
AST RIDING OF YORKSHIRE

1944—1974

by

E. A. ELTON

ational Administration
and History:
Monograph No. 2

Museum of the History of Education
University of Leeds
1974

Educational Administration and History: Monograph No. 2

SECONDARY EDUCATION
IN THE
EAST RIDING OF YORKSHIRE

1944—1974

by

E. A. ELTON

Museum of the History of Education
University of Leeds
1974

GENERAL EDITORS' NOTE

The Museum of the History of Education has in recent years been established as a centre for the illustration and investigation of the history of English education. To encourage research in this subject, and in the allied field of educational administration, the *Journal of Educational Administration and History* has been published in association with the Museum twice a year since 1968. It has become evident, however, that there still remains a need for an outlet for studies of a length falling between that of a journal article and a full-length book, and the present publication is the second of a series of monographs intended to appear periodically with the object of meeting such a need.

P. H. J. H. GOSDEN
W. B. STEPHENS
General Editors

L A
6 38
. y6 E48
1974

EDUCATIONAL ADMINISTRATION AND HISTORY MONOGRAPHS

No. 1. *Regional Variations in Education during the Industrial Revolution, 1780-1870: The Task of the Local Historian.*
by W. B Stephens. 1973.

No. 2. *Secondary Education in the East Riding of Yorkshire, 1944-1974.*
by E. A. Elton. 1974.

2

SECONDARY EDUCATION IN THE
EAST RIDING OF YORKSHIRE, 1944-1974

On 8th November, 1943 the Chairman of the East Riding Education Committee, the Secretary for Education and two other members of the Committee attended a conference of L.E.A. representatives in York. It was an occasion of some importance. One of the speakers was the Rt. Hon. R. A. Butler, President of the Board of Education. He addressed the assembly on the government's White Paper on Educational Reconstruction. [1] The delegation returned to Beverley clearly impressed by what the President had said. Together with the other members of the Education Committee they made it their business to get down to studying the new Education Bill. [2] One cannot help but be impressed by the sense of urgency displayed by the East Riding councillors during these months. They wasted little time in setting up an eight-man Educational Reconstruction Sub-Committee and soon appeared to grasp the essentials of the impending legislation.

At that time, the administration was limited both in size and in expertise. The Secretary for Education was not a trained schoolmaster and his deputy had no recognised qualifications. They were, together with a graduate inspector of schools, the chief local paid officials concerned with the administration of education in the East Riding. [3] The Reconstruction Sub-Committee was clearly concerned about the burden of work the new legislation would impose upon the Secretary. He was soon due to retire so it was decided to secure a successor as soon as possible. From a short-list of six, the Committee chose Victor Clark, Chief Education Officer for Doncaster and formerly Assistant Director for Northumberland, to be the new Chief Education Officer for the East Riding. [4] The job of chief local administrator was entirely recast by the 1944 Act. The statutory obligation 'secondary education for all' was to differentiate the work of the new East Riding chief officer from that of his predecessor in no lesser degree than it was to differentiate the rôle of President of the Board from that of the newly-appointed Minister for Education.

In 1944 the East Riding 'provision for secondary education consisted of four grammar schools and three senior elementary schools. For an able educationist, with a deep faith in the educability of the ordinary child [5] the East Riding appointment offered immense scope. Of the four grammar schools, two were aided and two were provided by the L.E.A. Beverley Grammar School, an ancient foundation, had been put on its feet by the Charity Commissioners in 1890 after twelve years of inactivity. Similarly, Bridlington School, had 'died from sheer penury and indifference' [6] and was re-established in 1899. In 1905 the new County Education Authority made a long-overdue contribution to secondary education for girls by providing Bridlington High School; in 1907 it went further and provided Beverley High School. Until 1944 these four grammar schools had mainly fee-paying pupils. As a condition of receiving government grant they were providing 25 per cent free places to children from public elementary schools.

The East Riding was not 'cluttered up with imitation secondary schools'. [7] There were two county senior schools at Hessle and Withernsea and one other shared with the Part III authority, Bridlington. [8] At Withernsea, where population growth had followed the coming of the railway and the fashion for holidays by the sea, there was scope for secondary education to develop unfettered by tradition. (The old grammar school at Halsham had irrevocably joined the ranks of the elementary schools by 1867). In 1921, with the population of Withernsea nearly five thousand, the county council acted to provide a separate senior department. This school soon began to attract considerable numbers of eleven year olds from the neighbouring villages. Here, in embryo, was the future comprehensive school.

For the majority of East Riding children elementary education was a relatively uninterrupted process from five to fourteen. [9] There are a number of possible explanations for this meagre provision in the inter-war years. First, there was no statutory obligation requiring local authorities to make such provision. 'Secondary education was still a voluntary matter, parents could not demand it as of right for their children and authorities were not obliged to spend even up to the limit of the two penny rate on 'education other than elementary.' [10] Secondly, in the absence of a national policy and central government direction, local initiative was important. Without pressure from a dynamic education officer, it was not difficult for a strong chairman to prevail upon the Education Committee and to slow down educational advance. Thirdly the East Riding could, with some justification, claim that its financial resources did not make possible more than a minimum provision of separate secondary schools. Yet how far this was an attitude of mind, a hangover from the days of the Geddes Axe, is difficult to determine. As A. J. P. Taylor has succinctly put it, 'the economies were soon undone. The arguments which accompanied them left a permanent mark'. [11]

What follows is an attempt to examine and in a modest way to assess the progress of secondary education in the East Riding since the great Education Act of 1944. The essay is largely administrative in orientation and there is no attempt to discuss the work of individual schools. There are many deficiencies, glaring ones perhaps to those more intimately involved with the work of local government.

The Development Plan

On taking up his appointment at the beginning of September 1944 the new Chief Officer was faced with the immediate task of implementing the demands of the 1944 Act which had become law on the 4th of August. Not only was the task a formidable one, there was a sense of urgency about the new measure. Section 11 laid down that within a year of the coming into operation of Part II of the Act (1st April, 1945) every local education

4

authority had to prepare and submit to the Minister a development plan showing what the authority proposed to do to secure that there should be 'sufficient' primary and secondary schools in its area, and how they proposed to do it.

Whatever the C.E.O. may have wanted to do for East Riding children, he was to some extent constrained by policies and attitudes within his own Education Committee and the Ministry of Education. [12] Although party politics has played a negligible part in local government in the East Riding, its representatives were not the sort to approve any new-fangled theories involving radical change without good reason. The East Riding's grammar schools were highly prized and any attempt to alter either their character or status would have been fiercely resisted.

Government policy in the mid 1940s has yet to be fully explored. [13] Available evidence suggests that the Coalition and post-war governments were strongly in favour of a tripartite system of secondary schools as advocated by the Spens Committee (1938) and the Norwood Committee (1943). The former had a good deal to say about the multilateral school but preferred not to advocate its general adoption on the grounds that it 'would be too subversive a change to be made in a long established system'. [14] The Norwood Committee treated with reverence some currently fashionable psychology and its Report appears to have had a powerful influence. As one early contributor to the literature on the comprehensive school has pointed out, 'secondary school organization at this vital period (1945-51) was befogged and bedevilled by the tremendous hold on almost all educationists which the movement for intelligence testing had acquired'. [15] Not everyone pressed for rigid conformity to these principles. The Spens Committee acknowledged that the multilateral idea was perhaps the right answer to the problems of sparsely populated areas. R. A. Butler expressed the hope that 'more than one type of secondary education may from time to time be amalgamated under one roof (so that) we may judge from experiments which is the best arrangement'. [16] Nonetheless, the incoming post-war Labour administration did not appear to favour multilateral schools any more than had the outgoing Coalition. Ministry of Education pamphlet No. 1, 'The Nations Schools', recommended to L.E.A.s. a tripartite system of secondary schools— grammar, modern and technical— as the most appropriate way of implementing the 1944 reforms. In fact, 'No encouragement was given to the establishment of the multilateral school which the Labour Party had espoused at its 1942 conference. Nor did the election victory and the appointment of a Labour Minister of Education, Ellen Wilkinson, greatly alter the policy of the Ministry'. [17]

In view of the pressures both local and national, it is clear that if the C.E.O. found the tripartite system not to his liking then he was going to have to take a more subtle and less doctrinaire approach to the planning of a system of secondary schools. During the first twelve months of taking up his appointment, the Chief Officer set out, in the manner of a bishop on a visitation of his diocese, to acquaint himself at first hand with the

5

schools of the East Riding. The visitation was an essential preliminary to the enormous task of planning and reconstruction that was to occupy the C.E.O. for the next two or three years. The changes introduced by the 1944 Act meant that the days of the all-age elementary school were numbered. Some 80 per cent of children between the ages of 11 and 14 were in the senior classes of this type of school. All but 8 per cent left at the statutory leaving age of fourteen. This problem dominates the planning and provision of education for the next fifteen years. Nearly 6,000 children qualified for accommodation in secondary schools in 1945 (see Map 1).

The East Riding Development Plan is divided into seven sections. [18] Section 1 dealing with primary and secondary schools is by far the largest. The Riding was divided into sixteen school districts and each district analysed under the following headings:

1. Number of pupils in the district on the registers of grant-aided schools on the last school day before 1st April, 1945.

2. Anticipated local changes (if any) likely to affect the child population of the school district.

3. Existing grant-aided primary and secondary schools maintained and/or proposed to be maintained by the authority.

4. Existing primary and secondary schools not maintained by the authority, but forming part of the local school provision.

5. Primary and secondary schools to be discontinued.

6. Proposed new primary and secondary schools to be maintained by the authority.

7. Arrangements to be made for meeting the needs of pupils who have not attained the age of five years.

The planners had to indicate those areas where possible future development might affect the child population—no easy task. Of the sixteen school areas, nine were considered to have the most likely growth prospects. Of the nine, four in close proximity to the boundary of the county borough of Kingston-upon-Hull, were expected to grow at a fairly fast rate. The seaside resorts, Bridlington, Hornsea and Filey, appeared likely to attract new residents. It was noted that at Filey a large holiday camp was being developed and at Brough a large aircraft factory was expanding.

Decision-making of this kind, together with an assessment of the condition of local elementary schools [19] was to be of paramount importance in determining priorities for future building programmes. Two other factors made planning for the future extremely difficult—the need to forecast the birth rate and the trend towards remaining at school beyond the statutory leaving age. For an overall view of the future of secondary education in the East Riding as adumbrated in the Development Plan, see Map 2. New secondary schools were envisaged as follows. Up to 17 schools to be developed as Modern/Technicals; possibly two new Grammar schools; three Secondary Modern schools; one (possibly two) Multilateral schools. The novel proposal was to cover the East Riding with bilateral schools. The Reconstruction Sub-Committee was thoroughly cautious about types of secondary school. 'It is dangerous at this stage', the members argued, 'for educationists to mesmerize themselves with

6

educational statistics and for education authorities to lay down hard and fast rules as to the character and type of this or that secondary school'.[20] The Committee felt that they would inevitably make mistakes but that time and experience rather than current educational fashion would enable them to be put right. Some authorities were experiencing real difficulties. In response to repeated requests for some indication of official policy, Sir John Maud put out a circular.[21] It appeared on the eve of publication of the East Riding Draft Plan. The Ministry pointed out that while it was 'inevitable for the immediate purposes of planning and in the light of existing schools, for local education authorities at the outset to think in terms of three types and to include information of the amount of accommodation allocated to each type in the development plan', it was not contemplated that this separate classification of schools would be irrevocable nor was there anything in the Education Act to suggest that it should be. On the contrary, it was felt that as time went, the conception of 'secondary schools' of varying curricula and age-ranges might well, through the development of the modern school, gradually replace the classification of schools into grammar, technical and modern.

The East Riding Chief Officer appears to have had good liaison with the Ministry and his views did not diverge fundamentally from those at the centre. There is nothing in the East Riding Plan which violated the guide lines set out by the Ministry either in 'The Nations Schools' or in Circular 73. Realistically, the latter document observed that 'the precise ways in which different types of education can best be combined and the details of planning bilateral and multilateral schools must depend on local circumstances'. But, at the same time the Minister reminded L.E.A.s that 'the organisation must not be such as to prejudice the position of other maintained secondary schools in the area'.

The following general principles were to apply to all the new East Riding secondary schools. As far as possible they were to provide for no less than 300 pupils, i.e. a minimum annual entry of at least two forms. Secondly, they were to offer a variety of courses and heads were to be encouraged to experiment to satisfy the needs of their pupils. Thirdly, pre-agricultural courses were recommended for the upper forms of rural secondary schools, and such courses were to be 'intimately associated with whatever Farm Institute provision may be made in the County'.[22]

The Draft Plan made provision for the improvement and adaptation of the four grammar schools. Following the Loveday Committee recommendations, heads of these schools were to feel free to introduce pre-agricultural courses or to promote an alternative form of secondary education where this was 'calculated to meet the needs of the area'.[23] For a number of years the East Riding would be dependent upon the use of selective secondary schools in neighbouring authorities to augment its provision for this 10 per cent to 15 per cent of the school population. In the Pocklington area arrangements were made for a large number of selected pupils to take up places at the direct grant school. Here, and at a number of other direct grant schools outside the authority, it was possible to make provision for a small number of boarders. For some children, especially those living in the remoter parts of the East Riding, boarding was essential. The Bridlington grammar schools already had boarding facilities which could be developed and extended. The Plan held out the possibility of additional boarding at Driffield if the proposed Modern and Technical (Agricultural) Secondary School developed as it was hoped. [24]

A special meeting of the Reconstruction Sub-Committee, held on 3rd January, 1946, made the following recommendations:

1. That the proposals for the establishment of new secondary schools and the continuance or adaptation of existing secondary schools as shown in the plan be adopted in principle.

2. That the County Architect be asked to prepare the necessary estimates and that steps be taken to appoint an architect to work exclusively in the educational service.

3. That immediate steps be taken with a view to acquiring sites for the proposed new secondary schools.

4. That in framing the programme of capital expenditure priority be given to the provision of the proposed new secondary schools.

5. That a copy of the Draft Development Plan be forwarded to the Ministry of Education.

This was an important meeting. It set in motion a great deal of activity in the interest of educational expansion in the East Riding of Yorkshire.

Although it has been suggested that there was nothing in the Plan to violate the Ministry's guidelines, the proposal to cover the East Riding with bilateral schools was novel and could expect to receive thorough scrutiny from the Ministry. Shortly after the Draft had been submitted, Labour Minister of Education, Ellen Wilkinson, issued what was to be her last circular on the subject. [25] She reminded L.E.A.s that plans were due by 1st April and suggested that in view of the difficulties, county authorities in particular might like to submit their plans by instalments. The Minister made clear that 'in general' she still adhered to the principles set out in 'The Nation's Schools'. With those authorities in mind, which were considering a general system of bilateral or small multilateral schools, she drew attention to the four basic principles in Circular 73 and in particular paragraphs 8(a) and (b). Whilst acknowledging that no hard and fast line could be drawn between Grammar, Technical and Modern educational provision, the Minister made clear that any proposals to deal with technical education alongside 'grammar' or 'modern' education in the same school would be carefully scrutinized to ensure that there was adequate scope for development and experiment. Proposals involving a 'technical' stream within a grammar school, for instance, by the mere addition of one or more practical rooms, were not likely to be approved. [26] As far as secondary technical education was concerned, the most important factor seems to have been the need to insist that local education authorities provided 'adequate scope for [its] development and experiment'. It could hardly have been otherwise, for as the preamble to the Berkshire Development Plan pointed out (and this applied equally to the East Riding) 'the technical requirements of a rural county which in 1945 had no technical provision cannot in the nature of the case be forecast with accuracy'.[27]

Although the Minister may have complimented the East Riding for submitting a draft plan well ahead of many other authorities, there can be little doubt that early in 1946, the C.E.O. and the Chairman of the Education Committee were summoned to the Ministry to defend the principles which they had outlined on paper. Three areas relating to secondary school provision appear most likely to have required detailed clarification—the nature and extent of grammar school provision, the so-called modern-cum-technical schools and the future for technical education at this level.

On paper the grammar-school provision was adequate, in so far as it matched the 10 per cent to 20 per cent recommended by the government. In the short term, however, some of these places would have to be taken up in schools outside the authority, at Malton, York, Selby, Drax, Goole and Hull. Only at Driffield and Hessle were new grammar schools envisaged. The Withernsea area, in the remoter part of Holderness, would have to be treated differently. Here, a well-established senior school had, since pre-war days, been evolving a fifth form and preparing pupils for external examinations. The headmaster, according to an unpublished article in the Beverley County Library, had been restrained by the authority from attempting to retain pupils beyond the age of fifteen in order to prepare them for matriculation. The new Chief Officer wanted this school to retain its grammar-school pupils and to provide both technical and general courses. The East Riding planners described it as a combined secondary school and must have felt confident that it fell well within the Spens' definition of an area suited to the development of a multilateral school.

The term 'bilateral' does not appear in the plan but for convenience it will now be used to refer to the large number of schools the authority proposed to develop as modern and technical schools. The Chief Officer's preference for such schools appears to have derived from a combination of ideological and practical considerations—his lack of faith in a modern school of limited conception and his good fortune in being able to plan for the future in an area noticeably deficient in secondary schools. Modern schools do appear in the plan, but of necessity, at Sledmere and Market Weighton where numbers seemed unlikely to exceed a two-form entry. In the case of the favourably located schools in Beverley and Driffield it was proposed to offer more specialised technical instruction. Two schools were to have an agricultural bias and one at Beverley was to offer commercial and industrial courses.

Although the C.E.O. may well have impressed Ministry officials with his understanding of the problems of promoting technical education in a rural area (his appointment to the Loveday Committee in 1948 suggests that he commanded respect in this field) it seems unlikely that he would have been able to report back to the education committee unqualified approval of the Plan. His unwillingness to think in terms of separate modern and technical schools can have earned him few friends at that time.

The North Riding Education Committee's experience under these circumstances is observable and some reference to it may help to clarify the issues.[28] The North Riding Plan was not submitted until 28 March, 1947. It was returned to Northallerton with a request for some drastic modifications. One of the Minister's main objections was to the tacking on of a technical stream to a small modern or grammar school and then labelling it as 'bilateral'. The Minister (then George Tomlinson) made an effort to clarify the position regarding secondary technical education in June of the same year.[29] He would not approve a secondary technical school or side within a secondary school which provided for less than 150 pupils of one sex. This effectively destroyed the North Riding's plans for one form entry technicals for boys and girls. It was not so much a question of not being allowed to make some provision for technical education but it did, as the North Riding had discovered, 'preclude the description of such schools as modern technical schools'. Specialized technical instruction—in agriculture, building, engineering, and commerce—had to be focused in a limited number of centres, viz. Northallerton, Scarborough, Eston, Redcar, Middlesbrough and York. The North Riding Plan was also roughly handled with regard to proposals for small multilateral or comprehensive schools: at Malton (630 mixed), Pickering (640 mixed), Thirsk (620 mixed) and Stokesley (600 mixed). In each case, the Minister required separate provision to be made for technical education.

The case of Malton is interesting because it brought the East Riding scheme into conflict with that of the North Riding. The North Riding Secretary for Education and his committee had had their proposal for a new multilateral at Malton rejected. The Minister, having listened to objection to this plan, preferred to retain the grammar school at Malton and to extend it, and to provide in addition, a new modern school. The North Riding Secretary has explained this decision and why the East Riding had to be consulted:[30]

> The governors of Malton Grammar School formally objected to the plan to provide a four form-entry grammar, technical and modern school at Malton, as the East Riding plan provided for a three form-entry technical and modern school at Norton, and they felt that the arrangement would make an invidious distinction between Malton and Norton. The Minister has met the objection to the extent of proposing that Malton in the North Riding and Norton in the East Riding shall each have a three form-entry modern school, one for boys and one for girls, each to serve the Malton and Norton areas; and that Malton Grammar School shall serve the North and East Riding areas now concerned and parts of the adjacent East Riding area.

The East Riding Chief Officer's influence in this matter may have been considerable. He did discuss the affair with the governors of Malton Grammar School and it was following these talks that the governors submitted their formal objection to the Minister, together with alternative proposals.[31] The interesting thing is that these proposals are almost identical to those later recommended by the Minister, with the exception that Malton was to continue to have a grammar school and not a grammar/technical.

This re-labelling of schools was quite acceptable to the East Riding. It would make little difference. The Chief Officer's attitude to the classification of secondary schools is clearly expressed in the 'First Five Years': [32]

> Although secondary schools, possibly for the sake of administrative convenience and out of regard to traditional nomenclature, might be labelled with particular titles, those labels should not necessarily determine what goes on inside the schools . . . the keynote of every secondary school, whatever it may be called in the first instance, will be flexibility, variety and freedom to experiment.

Flexibility, especially in the administrative sense, was very important because the C.E.O. aimed to integrate provision for the part-time education of 15 to 18 year olds within the framework of the new secondary schools. Like Henry Morris, he believed in providing in one building 'an organisation which would meet as many of the social and educational needs of the County as possible'. [33]

The East Riding Draft Plan reached the Minister's desk early in 1946, but it did not receive final approval until December 1948. [34] During this period, the plan was subjected to various observations, comments and criticisms. Even as late as 6 June, 1948 the C.E.O. was informed that although in general the Development Plan met 'with admirable suitability the needs of the authority's very rural area' the Minister required further information in certain details of the plan, particularly with regard to nursery provision and technical education. This ministerial nagging had gone on long enough. Within the Education Committee there were signs of irritation and impatience: [35]

> *Resolved.* That the C.E.O. reply to the Ministry, stating particularly that the authority will meet their obligations with regard to nursery provision and that they adhere to the view that secondary technical education should be provided in combination with secondary modern schools.

It is hardly surprising that some of the decisions taken then would not stand the test of time. As the Chief Officer pointed out there would be an inevitable time lag before the new educational prospect could be realised but this very factor would ultimately produce a greater reality about what at that moment was but 'the paper planning of some indication of the educational shape of things to come'. [36] Of the country as a whole it has been said that 'much of the forecasting was inaccurate, the pattern of population growth and movement proving to be different from what was expected'. [37] To say no more would be to belittle the undertaking. It was over 70 years since the state had set out to fill up gaps in elementary provision. In 1944, with powers vastly augmented, the state made clear that it had similar objectives, i.e. to provide all children between the ages of 11 and 15 with some form of schooling which could genuinely be described as secondary. Herein lies the importance of this now historic document.

The raising of the school leaving age on 1 April 1947 created an additional problem in secondary school administration which required an immediate solution. This long-overdue legislation required local education authorities to make immediate provision for all secondary school children to remain at school until the age of fifteen. In the East Riding detailed preparations were made and presented to the Education Committee twelve months before the event was due to take place.[38] Many children would have to transfer to larger 'central' schools for their extra year. Most of these centres were too small to take the extra numbers and had it not been for the rescue operation mounted by the Ministry of Education in conjunction with the Ministry of Works in making available H.O.R.S.A. teaching rooms, the new measure could not have been put into effect.[39]

Thus began 'the daily migration', which as Dr. Bamford observed, was soon to become 'the way of life of most country children of secondary school age, and indeed for most primary school children in rural areas'.[40] Methods of transporting the children to and from school were to be many and varied—contract bus, public bus service, taxi, cycle and even contract van. Nine Haltemprice children had to cycle from the villages of Dunswell and Skidby to school in Cottingham. The Education Committee voted them £1 each per annum for cycle wear and tear! An even more arduous journey faced five fourteen year olds from the village of Wawne. To get to school they had to cross the River Hull by ferry, then walk a mile to catch a bus to take them to Beverley. Not all children could be accommodated in the makeshift centres. There were 33 schools for which no special provision could be made. This meant that for the time being some 220 children had to stay on for the extra year in their small all-age schools. It was a question of doing what was possible under the very difficult circumstances of the immediate post-war years. In the words of the C.E.O. 'these modest concentrations afforded a better alternative than that of allowing boys and girls of the age of fourteen to remain in small village schools with no facilities for practical instruction and little in the way of contact with teachers trained to meet the needs of pupils of secondary school age'.[41]

A great many new schools had been planned but when they could be built was another question. The tone of Ministry circulars in 1945 appeared to rule out an early start on major building projects. This was the first, and perhaps the worst, of the three periods of post-war school building as defined in Ministry of Education pamphlet No. 33.[42] It was a time of general austerity, shortages of labour and materials, and complicated further by the raising of the school-leaving age, an increase in the birth rate and the need to provide schools in new housing areas. In 1945, therefore, the Education Committee made plans to patch up and adapt.[43]

Circular 122 appears to have taken the East Riding completely unawares. The Chief Officer commented, 'the position appears to be radically changed' and he expressed surprise that 'the Ministry should be prepared now to consider projects which a few months ago it was understood they could not entertain'. [44] Two major projects were submitted for 1947, one for a rural secondary school at Market Weighton, the other for an urban secondary school at Beverley. An ambitious list of twenty-two projects was submitted for the period 1947-53. This was too optimistic in view of building restrictions and it had to be reduced by almost a half.

When the Draft Development Plan was submitted to the Ministry in November 1946, it had included details of capital expenditure for the 1947-53 building programme. This did not satisfy the Minister. She wanted to know about the phasing and costing of the remainder of the programme for the years after 1953. The C.E.O. was not impressed and let his views be known. He 'informed the official concerned at the Ministry that with present day uncertainties, not excluding the possibility of boundary revision, he regarded the presentation of such information at this stage as a somewhat academic and unreal pursuit and that he would prefer to apply himself to present real and urgent tasks'. [45] However, working on the assumption that the Minister wished to proceed with the remainder of the heavy building programme in accordance with the rate of capital expenditure already approved for the years 1947-53, he concluded that up to £2,200,000 of building could be done in each five yearly period after 1953. This meant that the whole of the Development Plan could be put into effect by 1972-73. The total estimated cost of the entire capital programme was put at over £10 million. Of this, about £3½ million was committed to the programme for 1947-53. The remaining £7½ million was to be spread over the years 1953-1973. Spending on secondary schools was expected to account for more than half of the total figure. [46]

Primary Schools	...	£4,483,730
Secondary Schools	...	£5,220,906
Special Schools	...	£ 370,275

In making these submissions, the C.E.O. guardedly observed that 'a programme of this nature and over such a period of years must be regarded as only provisional and liable to re-adjustment as circumstances at the time may determine'.

Three important developments in the late 1940s were to have a significant effect upon school building. Forward planning of school building programmes began in 1947. L.E.A.s were asked to submit proposals for the calendar year 1949. Secondly, more detailed minimum standards were introduced from 1949 and thirdly a limit was imposed on the cost of schools based on an amount per place provided. [47] These have been 'the three essential features of all post-war building programmes since 1950'. [48]

The forward planning requirement descended upon L.E.A.s in the shape of Circular 155. The East Riding submission for 1949 building produced a conflict of outlook over priorities. [49] The Ministry examined the East Riding proposals and advised the inclusion of two colleges of further education, for Beverley and Bridlington. The C.E.O. was invited to

13

comment upon this recommendation. He was clearly not pleased and produced a list of eleven 'priorities', including five new secondary schools. With some reluctance he included the Beverley College of Further Education, a project which might not have been included at this stage had not his attention been drawn to Ministry Circular 180 which stressed the 'need for more provision for technical education in the interests of industrial efficiency and the economic well-being of the country'. The Chief Officer insisted that other local needs were more pressing. The East Riding situation was being aggravated by the recent rise in the birth rate, uncertainties over housing developments and the unexpected arrival in the county of groups of children of soldiers formerly serving abroad. The position was so complex that 'the influx of a few more children . . . might well make it necessary for the Education Committee to ask the Minister to agree to the submission of additional projects'.

This tough line appears to have been effective. The Minister agreed to the deletion of the Beverley and Bridlington Colleges of Further Education from the 1949 programme but requested that an early start be made on these colleges in 1950.[50] The Education Committee, sensing victory, now assumed an almost dictatorial stance. The following resolutions[51] were to be brought to the Minister's notice:

1. That the Authority remain convinced that despite the country's need for improved facilities for further Education, the educational interests of the East Riding will best be served by high priority being given to the building of new secondary schools during the next few years.

2. That bearing this in mind the Authority cannot undertake to start building two Colleges of Further Education during 1950, but they will ask the Educational Reconstruction Sub-Committee to determine which of the two Colleges shall be included in the programme for that year.

Surveying the progress made by 1950,[52] the Chief Education Officer acknowledged that things were not going as well as had been hoped. Despite this, there was one real foretaste of the educational shape of things to come with the completion of Longcroft County Secondary School, Beverley—the first of the new bi-laterals. This building complied with Ministry building regulations of 1945, which prescribed minimum and not maximum standards. For this reason, some of the post-war schools were found to be 'very extravagant both of land and floor space'.[53] From 1945 to 1949 building costs rose steadily, although there were marked regional variations. This, combined with the country's worsening economic position by mid 1949, made it necessary to introduce new building regulations and a limit on cost per place. The regulations issued in 1951 and 1954 reduced the minimum area of teaching accommodation for a three form-entry secondary school by 2,356 square feet. Cost per place limits became operative for projects in the 1950-51 programme. This amounted to a reduction of about 12½ per cent on the average cost which meant for secondary pupils £290 per place instead of around £320. The new measure was to enable work to continue at the same rate but at a substantially lower cost. In short, The 'pursuit of value for money can be said to date from this moment'.[54]

14

The Beverley school had been well-planned and lavishly equipped. It was obviously important to the C.E.O. to have a show-piece in the capital of the East Riding and to let it be known as widely as possible that this was really a sort of educational stone-laying ceremony for the newly-planned edifice of secondary schooling for the East Riding. For the big occasion, a glossy programme was prepared and Sir John Maud, chief executive officer at the Ministry of Education, was invited to perform the opening ceremony. The 53 acre Longcroft site was not relatively expensive but the building was.[55] The new building regulations of 1951 ushered in a new era in school building. In future, less circulation space would be provided. It could no longer be provided generously and in splendid isolation but had to be incorporated in, or used in conjunction with the teaching space, 'so as to increase the amount of useful floor space without increasing the total size of the building'.[56] Much more information was made available to local authorities in the 1950s on the design, building and equipping of schools as a result of the work of the Ministry of Education Development Group. A secondary modern school for 600 boys and girls was built in 1951 for the Berkshire authority, pioneering new ideas put out by the Ministry. The net cost per place worked out at as little as £215·3.[57] Significantly, the East Riding's second new secondary school, a four form-entry school at Cottingham, which opened in 1955, cost nearly a third less than the expensive Beverley school.[58]

Forward planning continued to present difficulties. The C.E.O. pointed out[59] that as regards the next five years, 1950-54, the Ministry could not be supplied with the information it required until the Education Department was in possession of more up-to-date information from the housing authorities and had been able to undertake further research into birth statistics. The 1950 building programme comprised five projects, four of which were for new secondary schools. It had to be drastically reduced and not in the way suggested by the C.E.O. The Minister approved only the two projects for Hessle: a new infant and junior school and the adaptation of a Georgian mansion to provide the nucleus for a new secondary school. Perhaps the inclusion of a college of further education would have produced a more favourable response!

Building cuts continued well into the 1950s. In a memorandum on the subject,[60] the C.E.O. pointed out that owing to the shortage of steel and temporary overloading of the building industry, any major work in the 1951-52 programme which was not started by 4th February, 1952 would have to be deferred. The Minister called for a revised building programme for 1952-53 to be drawn up from the balance of work in the 1951-52 programme and that in the programme for 1952-53.

The evolution of the East Riding building programme is outlined in Appendix III. It was not until 1963 when the new secondary schools at Fulford and Norton received their first entry of pupils that 'secondary education for all' as envisaged in the 1944 Act, was accomplished in the East Riding of Yorkshire.

'By 1964, 71 per cent of all authorities either had, or intended to establish, some form of comprehensive education.'[61] The East Riding had at this time two established comprehensive schools. A decision to allow two more secondary schools to develop on comprehensive lines prompted one member of the Education Committee to enquire how far this was in accordance with the Committee's policy for secondary education in the East Riding. It was decided to refer 'this important matter' to the Secondary and Further Education Sub-Committee and in October of the same year, the C.E.O. published a memorandum on the subject.[62] This is an interesting policy discussion, appearing as it does on the eve of the Labour government's accession to power and the promulgation of Circular 10/65.

The C.E.O. assembled some impressive evidence (Tables 1 and 1A) which suggested that the existing organisation of secondary education was 'accompanied by high and, possibly outstanding achievement'. The Education Committee had to decide whether it wished to continue the existing pattern or to change it. The Committee played safe. The two or three proposed comprehensives were approved but only in so far as this was quite in keeping with the policy of maintaining a variety of secondary schools related to the needs of the localities they served.[63]

TABLE 1
Number of Pupils remaining at school beyond statutory leaving age
Yorkshire Authorities as shown in Ministry of Education Statistics,
List 69 (January, 1963)

Authority	Pupils aged 15 years as a percentage of those aged 13 two years previously		Pupils aged 16 years as a percentage of those aged 13 three years previously		Pupils aged 17 years as a percentage of those aged 13 four years previously	
	Boys	Girls	Boys	Girls	Boys	Girls
Yorkshire, East Riding	51·1	52·7	29·1	28·4	13·2	12·2
Yorkshire, West Riding	32·3	30·7	19·3	18·2	11·0	9·1
Yorkshire, North Riding	32·1	29·3	17·8	16·0	10·7	9·8
Hull	30·4	27·7	16·4	13·5	9·2	7·1
Barnsley	25·5	24·8	13·2	12·2	6·7	8·4
Bradford	36·8	31·8	19·2	16·9	9·3	8·8
Dewsbury	33·0	29·0	20·3	15·8	9·4	6·3
Doncaster	40·6	30·4	23·7	20·6	17·2	10·1
Halifax	34·0	35·7	24·7	18·3	13·9	10·9
Huddersfield	38·2	34·0	18·9	12·0	10·0	8·3
Leeds	37·4	31·2	20·9	17·6	11·1	8·9
Middlesbrough	37·4	29·2	16·2	14·8	6·0	5·7
Rotherham	32·1	27·6	15·4	17·6	8·1	10·0
Sheffield	42·5	30·6	20·8	16·1	11·3	8·2
Wakefield	25·1	21·6	14·5	15·3	7·3	9·1
York	25·1	24·0	14·2	15·2	10·3	8·8

TABLE 1A

Awards made by Local Education Authorities for the Educational Year 1962-63

Yorkshire Authorities as shown in Ministry of Education Statistics, List 71 (1962)

	New University Awards per 1,000 pop. in age group		New Full Value Awards at other F.E. Establishments per 1,000 pop. in age group		New Students entering Training Colleges per 1,000 pop. in age group		Total Full Value Awards—including Training College Awards per 1,000 pop. in age group	
1.	Huddersfield	51·9	YORKS. EAST RIDING	35·2	Doncaster	51·8	YORKS. EAST RIDING	126·2
2.	York	43·6	Dewsbury	33·4	YORKS. EAST RIDING	48·2	Huddersfield	109·6
3.	YORKS. EAST RIDING	42·8	Hull	31·0	Huddersfield	45·0	Doncaster	107·8
4.	Leeds	36·4	Yorks. North Riding	29·0	Wakefield	39·9	Yorks. North Riding	101·3
5.	Yorks. North Riding	35·9	Yorks. West Riding	25·5	Rotherham	37·1	Dewsbury	96·5
6.	Sheffield	33·7	Doncaster	24·6	Yorks. North Riding	36·4	York	96·0
7.	Yorks. West Riding	32·3	York	23·8	Yorks. West Riding	34·9	Yorks. West Riding	92·7
8.	Doncaster	31·4	Leeds	22·7	Dewsbury	33·4	Wakefield	89·1
9.	Bradford	30·8	Wakefield	21·1	Halifax	32·6	Leeds	83·2
10.	Halifax	30·4	Sheffield	13·4	Barnsley	32·5	Hull	77·7
11.	Dewsbury	29·7	Barnsley } Huddersfield	12·7	Middlesbrough	29·2	Rotherham	72·8
12.	Wakefield	28·1	Bradford	11·5	Bradford	28·7	Barnsley	71·3
13.	Barnsley	26·1	Rotherham	10·2	York	28·6	Sheffield	71·1
14.	Rotherham	25·5	Halifax	6·7	Leeds	24·1	Bradford	71·0
15.	Middlesbrough	25·0	Middlesbrough	6·3	Sheffield	24·0	Halifax	69·7
16.	Hull	22·8			Hull	23·9	Middlesbrough	60·5
	Average for all 49 English County Authorities	33·4		23·1		27·2		83·7

17

Significant changes in educational thinking during the late 1950s and early 1960s had accelerated the trend towards comprehensive schooling. The popular mood of the '60s was such that 'few were prepared to argue against stronger government leadership and intervention in education'.[64] The arguments of educational psychologists and sociologists carried considerable weight. Serious doubts were cast upon the reliability and validity of intelligence testing and evidence that access to the more favoured forms of education was differentiated according to social class began to accumulate in official reports. More important, perhaps, from the government's point of view were the arguments advanced by respected economists that educational expenditure should be regarded as economic investment.

It was against this background that the Labour Secretary of State for Education and Science issued Circular 10 of 1965 which stated inter alia that it was the government's objective 'to end selection at eleven plus and to eliminate separatism in secondary education'.

The Secretary of State accordingly requested the L.E.A.s, if they had not already done so, to prepare and submit plans for reorganising secondary education in their areas on comprehensive lines. No rigid formula was prescribed. The Minister considered six possibilities and of these four were regarded as being entirely acceptable to the government. No legislation accompanied 10/65, but local education authorities were asked to submit their schemes within one year of the issue of the Circular. The Minister's approach over this matter has been described as 'collaborative, experimental, even cautious'.[65] L.E.A.s were encouraged to sound out the feelings of parents and teachers and the policy document did not preclude variety and experiment in organisational patterns.

The East Riding proposals were published late in the same year in the form of a memorandum by the C.E.O.[66] The Chief Officer wisely sought to defuse the issue by pointing out that whatever long-term and short-term plans were submitted, building costs would ensure that the existing system would inevitably persist for several years because the Circular was 'reticent on the matter of money'. He maintained, however, that whether Circular 10/65 had been issued or not, the time was coming when L.E.A.s in general must feel the need to review their organisation of secondary education and to determine what steps could be taken to get rid of eleven plus selection and the consequent disunity which it imposed within the educational system. He had given his own Education Committee the opportunity to take this step the previous year but it had been reluctant to do so. Now, with Ministry approval, the C.E.O.'s hand was considerably strengthened.

Of the four types of comprehensive organisation most strongly advocated in the Circular, the school with an age range 11 to 18 commended itself to the East Riding Education Committee. The progress of Withernsea High School had been watched with interest for nearly twenty years and it had an excellent record of achievement. Four other schools were evolving along similar lines.[67] A major problem was how to accommodate within the scheme the relatively small grammar schools in Beverley and

Bridlington, which at that time could not be considered individually as viable comprehensive units. [68] A two tier system therefore seemed to offer a practical means of utilising the existing buildings. In this respect, Sixth Form Colleges were tempting, especially as the secondary schools at Hornsea and Filey had not yet developed sixth forms. The C.E.O. went so far as to suggest that a sixth form college would be 'an inevitable feature of any reorganisation along comprehensive lines'. [69] But the Circular had been guarded in its approval of this kind of reorganisation and for the time being the Minister was only prepared to permit a limited number of such experiments. A fourth possibility was the middle school. This 'novel form of primary-cum-secondary school', as the Chief Officer termed it, could take children at eight or nine and retain them until twelve or thirteen. Circular 10/65 was as guarded about this concept as it had been about the sixth form college and for two reasons the middle school idea was not likely to take root in the East Riding. Firstly, it was felt that such schools would not relate well to the existing medium-sized secondary schools and secondly, because of the effect it would have on some rural areas. Any proposal that might further reduce the number of village schools was likely to encounter the fiercest opposition. Since 1945 over seventy village schools in the East Riding had been closed. [70] Finally, the Authority's ties with voluntary-aided and direct grant schools would have to be reconsidered.

The long-term plan put to the Education Committee by its Chief Officer can be summarised as follows:

8 all-through 11-18 comprehensives: Withernsea, Hessle, Willerby, South Hunsley, South Holderness, Barlby, Driffield, Fulford and Woldgate (Pocklington).

2 two-tier schools (the top tiers with enlarged VIth form provision): the grammar schools at Beverley and Bridlington.

6 schools with 11-16 age range (with VIth form provision at Beverley, Bridlington and in the case of Howden, at Barlby and Norton, at Malton): Bridlington (Headlands) Cottingham, Filey, Hornsea, Howden and Norton.

1 Middle School (age range 9-13, pupils transferring to Woldgate): Market Weighton

Circular 10/65 did not offer any advice on how to incorporate the voluntary schools into schemes of reorganisation. Local authorities were asked to enter into negotiations with the governing bodies of aided and special agreement schools and with diocesan authorities so as to bring the affected schools into an integrated scheme. The position of the direct grant schools was dealt with in one brief paragraph. The Secretary of State hoped that L.E.A.s would study ways in which the schools might be associated with their plans and that governing bodies would be ready to consider changes in curriculum, in method and age of entry which would enable them to participate fully in the local schemes. [71] At the same time the Labour government set up a Commission to advise upon the best way of integrating the public schools into the state system of education. [72]

The East Riding had a long-standing arrangement with two direct grant schools, Hymers College (Hull) and Pocklington School. As far as Hymers was concerned, the Education Committee decided that it would be 'wise to leave this to be the concern of the Hull authority'.[73] Pocklington had a much closer relationship with the county and there was a natural reluctance to sever the connection. The school was situated within the East Riding and its headmaster was a co-opted member of the Education Committee. Twenty-five selected pupils were admitted each year and the total of county boys at the school in 1965 was 178. Without clarifying how the selection would be made, the C.E.O. suggested that a way out of the difficulty might be for the County to continue to send 25 pupils to Pocklington 'but on the understanding that, say, not more than three would come from the area from which any one of our maintained schools draws its pupils'.[74]

Circular 10/65 stated that governors of controlled and county schools as well as the teachers and their organisations should have the opportunity to comment upon any scheme of reorganisation. A copy of the draft proposals was sent to all the governors and heads of secondary schools and to the teachers' organisations. The usual procedure was for a governors' meeting to be held at which the C.E.O. or his representative would be invited to attend and to comment upon the draft proposals. The views of the head and governors would be heard and debated and any resolutions recorded in the minutes. A large majority of the governing bodies gave their support to the Authority's schemes of reorganisation.[75] Out of twenty-one governing bodies, only six objected. Of these, two were simply expressing a desire to develop their own sixth forms.[76] A major note of dissent came from Beverley Grammar School with lesser ones from Beverley High School, Bridlington High School and Market Weighton.

The governors of Market Weighton County Secondary School were reluctant to accept a scheme which involved all pupils over the age of thirteen being transferred to Woldgate Secondary School at Pocklington. In short, they were opposed to the idea of becoming a middle school.[77] The C.E.O. promised to look at other possibilities and undertook to seek the advice of the D.E.S. before reaching a final decision. It was very much a problem of numbers for even after the raising of the school leaving age, Market Weighton was only expected to have between 350 and 400 pupils.

The Bridlington High School objections were to some extent blunted because the two other Bridlington secondary schools were in broad agreement with the proposed changes. The High School for Girls had to face the most radical change—from single sex grammar to mixed comprehensive lower school. The governors desperately wanted the school to retain some of its old identity and to become an 11—18 comprehensive for girls.

The governors of both the Beverley grammar schools were opposed to reorganisation. The governors of the Girls' High School were disturbed at the prospect of the school becoming a co-educational lower school. They expressed a preference to be reorganised as a single sex comprehensive with an age range of 11 to 16. Beverley Grammar School fiercely contested the draft proposals. The governors of this voluntary aided secondary

20

school (the only one in the East Riding) published their arguments in favour of retaining the school as a selective grammar school.[78] They referred to 10/65 as 'an unwise, revolutionary scheme forced upon us from Whitehall' and described it as 'a leap in the dark'. They clearly would have preferred the local authority not to have collaborated with the government. The governors saw the L.E.A.'s proposals as a danger to the bright children and a threat to the less able. They pointed out that sixth form colleges were envisaged in the Crowther Report and were acceptable within the terms of Circular 10/65. In their opinion, such an arrangement would be practicable in Beverley and Bridlington and possibly elsewhere in the East Riding. Had not the C.E.O. himself proposed that all sixth form work in Bridlington should be concentrated in one school? Why not also in Beverley? The C.E.O. who had, in 1947, championed the cause of Malton Grammar School against a scheme for comprehensive reorganisation put forward by the North Riding[79] was not very sympathetic. He refuted the suggestion that it was his personal desire to remove the school's aided status. He explained that it was his wish that the governors should be aware of the financial implications of maintaining such a status. It could become a voluntary controlled school enjoying considerable independence without the embarrassment of fund raising. He also reminded them that as far as sixth form colleges were concerned there was far less experience of them than of comprehensive schools. Whilst still adhering to the view that the Authority's proposals offered the best solution he promised that the advice of the D.E.S. would be sought.

Although some differences of opinion emerged, the large majority of teachers in the East Riding appeared to favour a comprehensive system.[80] A questionnaire sent to all members of the East Riding Association of Headteachers brought replies from nearly three-quarters of them. Sixty-six per cent were in full agreement with the Authority's draft proposals. Only 4 per cent were against the principle of reorganisation. The Joint Four, reflecting the views of many graduate teachers especially those in the grammar schools, was critical of the proposals. Experience, it argued, had proved that the policy of the Education Committee (re-affirmed as recently as October 1964) of developing a variety of schools according to local circumstances, far from impeding children was raising educational standards and was providing unlimited opportunity for advancement. The Joint Four was particularly concerned about the schools in Beverley and Bridlington and made the following proposals: 1. That the two Beverley grammar schools be allowed to develop as single sex comprehensives. Alternatively, the boy's grammar school be allowed to develop as a co-educational sixth form centre. 2. The C.E.O.'s proposals for Bridlington, they observed, would 'radically change Bridlington School and destroy the High School'. These two schools should be allowed to develop as single-sex comprehensives. The National Association of School Masters was in broad agreement with the proposed reorganisation. Some fear was expressed that Filey should continue to lose its sixth formers to Bridlington. This it was felt would affect the prestige of the school and it would be

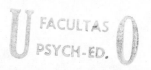

deficient in specialist staff, acommodation and equipment.[81] The East Riding County Association of the N.U.T. fully supported the move towards a complete system of comprehensive schools and the abolition of the eleven plus examination. It proposed that the direct grant schools, Pocklington and Hymers, be deprived of all state aid. The majority of members favoured two all-through comprehensive schools for Bridlington and were opposed to the idea of establishing a sixth form college. Neither did the N.U.T. favour the middle school proposal for Market Weighton, preferring the school to become an eleven to sixteen comprehensive.

The C.E.O. published a further memorandum which indicated that the Secretary of State had given general approval to the East Riding proposals.[82] Whilst accepting the form of organisation proposed for Bridlington, the D.E.S. pointed out that it was to be expected that the Headlands School would in course of time be ready to develop its own sixth form. In endorsing the Authority's proposal for Market Weighton the D.E.S. observed that this middle school would be unique in the county and that the Authority would no doubt watch its development with particular interest. With regard to Beverley, the D.E.S. acknowledged the difficulties but found the Authority's proposals entirely acceptable in principle. A sixth form college at Beverley was a non-starter for three reasons. Firstly, it was not the choice of the Authority. Secondly, the Beverley area could not in the near future hope to produce the desirable number of sixth form students, i.e. 350 to 400. Thirdly, it was not right to deprive other schools outside the Beverley area in order to make a sixth form college for Beverley a viable proposition.

Clearly the D.E.S. wanted no hasty moves over Beverley in the rather heated atmosphere that prevailed in 1967. In that year the legal basis for reorganisation was given a thorough testing. Enfield Grammar School governors successfully contested the Enfield Borough Council's attempt to end selection.[83] Two areas of the 1944 Act encouraged parents to contest in the courts any attempt to interfere with grammar schools. Section 76 implied a degree of parental choice and Section 13 required L.E.A.s to consult the public when intending to establish a new secondary school. A letter from the D.E.S. was obviously intended to deter the C.E.O. from implementing the Authority's interim scheme.[84]

To allay the fears of those who might have concluded that these were in any way final and irrevocable decisions the C.E.O. pointed out that the Secretary of State's 'blanket approval' did not at this stage indicate final approval of specific proposals. Furthermore, any proposal involving the major extension of a school or the amalgamation of schools would require publication of statutory notice in accordance with Section 13 of the 1944 Education Act. This would provide 'democratic opportunity for objection by the public in general or by governing bodies in particular'.[85]

In September 1963 the Education Committee was at last in a position to claim that every child in the East Riding over the age of eleven was attending a genuine, purpose-built secondary school.[86]

Progress in the field of secondary education had been reviewed at a conference of senior members of staff held in November, 1957 and a report of this meeting was presented to the Education Committee.[87] The C.E.O. reminded headteachers that he had rejected the so-called 'modern' school idea because in his view such a school would possess 'neither natural leaders, nor pupils of more than average ability'. 'So truncated an institution', he argued, would be 'colourless, unimaginative and limited in scope'. He would not therefore speak of modern schools, such an expression was 'taboo in the East Riding of Yorkshire'. There appeared to be sincere and unanimous aproval for the way the system was developing and it appeared to be beneficial in a number of ways—in recruiting staff, in its effects upon pupils and in enlisting the support and co-operation of the parents.

It was felt that staffing had been made easier because of a fairly generous system of allowances for heads of departments in the non-selective schools.[88] With the grammar school intake relatively static, more and more academically able children were being left to the general secondary schools, and these pupils, it was claimed, were proving to be the natural leaders of the school society and were capable of success in external examinations. Small sixth forms were being created in some schools because of the reluctance of some pupils to transfer to the grammar schools for advanced work. The C.E.O. in his report spoke of 'a perceptible change in the attitude of parents'. They appeared to be getting over the belief that failure at 'eleven plus' meant that the door to all forms of higher education was closed.[89] In addition to preparing some pupils for G.C.E. most schools were offering, on the technical side, courses leading to examinations conducted by the Northern Counties Technical Examinations Council, the Royal Society of Arts, the Union of Lancashire and Cheshire Institutes, and the Royal Horticultural Society. He made reference to the growing link between the rural secondary schools and the County Institute of Agriculture at Bishop Burton. There was a waiting list of pupils seeking entry to this branch of further education. The report did not have much to say about the less-gifted pupils but it was generally felt that they were encouraged and stimulated by the variety of work and opportunities being made available. The C.E.O. concluded in a manner which was intended to leave no one in doubt:

> The teachers and administrators who attended this conference certainly demonstrated their faith in the educability of the ordinary child and are persuaded that by their practice of a flexible and less dogmatic organisation of secondary education in place of the more conventional and rigid tripartite system, they may be exploiting reserves of undiscovered talent in their pupils and perhaps, also in themselves.

Having converted his teachers and the Education Committee, the Chief Officer must have felt completely vindicated when the Minister appeared at last to be taking his side.[90] There was a time, he observed, when the East Riding system of secondary schools did not 'find much favour in Curzon Street or with the H.M.I.s'. In fact, some H.M.I.s had advised that 'the attempt to provide a variety of courses for children of different abilities within one school was foredoomed to failure'. Still less encouragement had been received when it had been suggested that pupils other than those confined to grammar school should take external examinations including G.C.E. at ordinary level.[91]

The climate of opinion was indeed changing. In 1967, the Education Committee was able to record with pleasure and satisfaction, 'the warm tributes paid by H.M.I.s to the Authority and to the staffs of its general and comprehensive schools on the outstanding success of their Vth and VIth forms in particular, and their development in general throughout the post-war period'.[92] The growth of the Vth and VIth forms was indeed impressive as Table 2 indicates.

Table 2

School	Vth Form Established	Numbers	1967–8 Vth Formers	VIth Formers
Barlby...	1961	13	23	13
Longcroft	1950	22	142	61
Headlands	1954	51	113	29
Cottingham	1956	26	50	21
Driffield	1963	55	96	58
Filey	1962	32	34	—
Fulford	1964	5	47	17
Hornsea	1959	22	53	—
Howden	1962	21	26	—
Market Weighton ...	1955	10	29	—
Norton	1964	17	23	—
South Holderness ...	1955	30	71	19
South Hunsley ...	1958	41	62	10
Willerby	1961	33	94	47
Woldgate	1959	14	48	32
Hessle	1954	14	140	110
Withernsea	1923	6	115	114

In 1964, Ministry of Education statistics showed the East Riding to have the best record of all the Yorkshire authorities, borough and county, for numbers of pupils remaining at school beyond the statutory leaving age.[93] The Authority also topped the league in terms of 'Full Value Awards' for higher and further education.[94] Figures for the subsequent eight years have been equally impressive. Only recently has a serious attempt been made to interpret these statistics on a national or regional basis. Professor R. M. Rawstron has suggested that the data for the numbers of pupils in sixth forms in England and Wales reflects 'the opportunities available to children to make the most of their talents' and 'the degree to which

24

L.E.A.s are succeeding in their attempts to foster those talents efficiently'. [95] His analysis led him to conclude that 'as an individual authority, that of the East Riding may well be one of the most interesting and effective in the country as far as sixth form opportunities are concerned'. He also pointed out that it was remarkable that the East Riding was able to produce a greater number of sixth formers than Cheshire, Solihull or Bath, which were 'residentially wealthier places, well above the national average norm in their quota of top socio-economic groups'. 'Equally intriguing', he suggested, was 'why the East Riding should do so much better than similar agricultural counties like Norfolk, Cambridge and Ely'. [96]

Any discussion of the influence of environment upon educational performance in general terms is not likely to be very profitable. The following should, therefore, be regarded as only tentative and perhaps interesting observations. The East Riding was not a development area although as part of the Yorkshire and Humberside region it came under the scrutiny of the Hunt Committee. [97] This body examined those 'grey' areas where the rate of economic growth gave cause for concern. The problems facing the rural parts of Yorkshire and Humberside are less acute than those of the urban and industrial areas. Nevertheless, in the short term, the main problem both for Hull and its hinterland was to create 'sufficiently wide and diversified employment opportunities' and there was an immediate need for some help to be given to this area if its difficulties, 'isolation, poor communications and narrow range of employment', were to be overcome and the area's potential utilised. [98] The Hunt Committee made special reference to Bridlington and Filey and suggested that the economies of both towns were suffering primarily as a result of their over-dependence on the declining holiday trade. Economic problems such as these may well contribute to staying on at school and help to explain why from the northern counties as a whole a large proportion of sixth formers enter colleges of education. [99]

Taylor and Ayres have attempted an 'ecological approach' to the problem of educational opportunity. [100] In their view, 'the educational opportunity available to a child depends to a great extent on the variety and quality of education provided in the area in which he lives', and 'whether the quality is as good as it could be or whether the child derives maximum benefit depends upon a number of non-educational factors in the environment'. [101] Drawing heavily upon I.M.T.A. statistics, they make some attempt to discern regional variations. If, as they suggest, standards of housing are among the major environmental factors affecting children's health, education, and outlook on life, then East Riding children are relatively well off. It may also be significant that in 1966 the East Riding had to provide only 4·2 per cent of its children with free meals compared with 5·5 per cent West Riding, 6·6 per cent North Riding and 7·9 per cent Hull.

In terms of local authority income, the East Riding was not a rich authority. [102] Dividing the product of a 1d. rate for each L.E.A. by the number of children, Taylor and Ayres found that the average for counties

25

was 19s. 8d. On their calculations, the East Riding was 4s. below the average. This somewhat fragmentary evidence led them to suggest that 'if the proportion of children staying on at school and proceeding to university were the same in the impecunious as in the wealthy authorities, the impecunious would be near to insolvency'. [103] In fact, the East Riding had a record equal to that of the more prosperous county authorities, Cheshire and Surrey. [104]

One of the major factors influencing the quality of education in an area, suggest Taylor and Ayres, is the supply of teachers. Their analysis, using teacher salaries in primary schools, gave the East Riding an above-average record. [105] In 1965 East Riding primary schools were above the national average in terms of pupil-teacher ratios and size of classes. In England and Wales 12·4 per cent of classes had more than forty pupils on roll, while in the East Riding the figure was 2·7 per cent. The pupil/teacher ratio in the United Kingdom was 28·5 per cent against the 24·2 per cent. in the East Riding, while the figures for the average size of classes were 32·5 per cent and 27 per cent respectively. [106] In March 1964 there were noticeably fewer graduates in modern schools than in the other types of secondary schools (Table 3). [107]

Table 3

	Graduate teachers England & Wales (1964)	Graduate teachers East Riding
Modern	26·3 per cent	
Grammar	80·8 per cent	75·4 per cent
Technical	52·7 per cent	
Bilaterals & Comprehensives	55·0 per cent	49·8 per cent*

*(51·5 per cent if the bilaterals are considered separately)

Reference has already been made to the suggestion that a fairly generous system of allowances had helped to attract teachers. It has been the policy of the authority to minimise as far as possible any distinction in this respect between selective and non-selective schools. [108]

Although working in a predominantly rural area, East Riding teachers have been provided since 1945, with ample opportunities to keep in touch with up-to-date trends in educational thought and practice. A survey of courses provided for teachers in the East Riding was carried out over a period of three years by H.M. Inspectors. [109] Their report stated that 'when the Education Act of 1944 was published, the C.E.O. for the East Riding began immediately to consider its implications with regard to in-service training of teachers and others engaged in the Authority's educational service . . . with the full support of the Education Committee, the C.E.O. has, from 1945, been responsible for planning programmes of courses which, within the limits of the finance available, have ranged as widely as possible and have included many topics of vital importance to

26

the contemporary scene'. The inspectors maintained that in the overall planning of the courses, the wide experience and shrewd judgement of the C.E.O. was invaluable as also was his keen personal interest which impelled him 'to visit as many of the courses as his other duties [would] allow and to take a very active part in their intellectual and social proceedings'. They further pointed out that the choice of staff for the courses received very careful consideration, every effort being made to secure the services of experts from all spheres of educational activity.(110) In fact, the Authority had invited H.M. Inspectorate to participate in some of the courses, and those H.M.I.s with assignments of work in the East Riding were kept fully informed and were always welcome to attend. The report acknowledged that such contacts were 'of much value to the Inspectorate'.

An important factor in the successful development of secondary education has been the strong leadership and direction given to the schools and their administration by the Chief Education Officer until his retirement in 1971. The conference of administrators and senior members of staff of secondary schools already referred to is an excellent example of an important ingredient in his style of leadership. This strong leadership has strengthened and encouraged independence of thought and action in secondary school heads and their governing bodies. The schools have enjoyed a large measure of freedom to experiment. The C.E.O.'s qualities as an administrator are best seen in his dealings with his Education Committee and with the D.E.S. In the case of the former, he soon built up a reputation as a very skilled committee man. The formative years, 1945-50, enabled him to demonstrate his capabilities and to enhance his prestige in the eyes of his fellow administrators and elected representatives. The willingness of councillors to accept his views need not be regarded as weakness on their behalf but rather as a recognition of his expertise and knowledge. The Chief Officer has benefited from the absence of those political pressures which often create tensions in the large urban authorities and he has had little to contend with in the way of pressure groups.(111) The possibility of a serious clash of views within the Education Committee might have arisen, one would have thought, over comprehensive re-organisation. Yet this was not the case. The small murmurings of opposition on this highly emotive subject, made little headway against the combined strength of the C.E.O. and the Chairman of the Education Committee, Lady Halifax. The C.E.O.'s dealings with the Ministry, although difficult to appraise, do appear to exhibit the same characteristics of firmness and determination. Reference has already been made to his intransigence over the Development Plan in face of pressure from the Ministry and H.M.Inspectorate.(112) Likewise, he was prepared to fight hard over the content of a major building programme.(113)

Clearly, a much more intensive study is required. As Professor Rawstron was careful to observe, 'there is far more to educational efficiency than sixth forms and places at university and training colleges'.(114) For example, the East Riding did not spend heavily on primary education. Taylor and Ayres have shown that as far as expenditure per 100 pupils on primary school maintenance, repairs and furniture is concerned, the Authority appeared to be 10 per cent to 20 per cent below the average spending for counties.[115] A recent article[116] on the subject of spending by L.E.A.s on books, equipment and materials, drew attention to the wide disparity in levels of provision between different areas'. A league table of L.E.A. spending on learning resource materials was said to show the East Riding in both primary and secondary education to be amongst four other authorities 'jockeying for bottom place'. This charge was sufficient to draw fire from the new East Riding Chief Officer. In a short but fierce exchange of letters,[117] with charge and counter charge of misuse of statistics, he managed (with difficulty) to prove that the East Riding was in fact placed 31st and 33rd and not 56th and 58th as had been suggested.

In April 1967 H.M. Inspectorate was asked to complete a return for each L.E.A. in England outside the Greater London area, showing the view which the Inspectorate had taken of an Authority's performance and with regard to the education service as a whole.[118] The Inspectors were asked to make their judgements without reference to the particular size and circumstances of the authority, but their gradings were later related to the population size of the L.E.A.s. Although the Maud findings confirmed that the larger authorities tended also to be the more efficient, there were seven Grade 2 or 'good' authorities amongst the counties with populations between 200,000 and 400,000. Maud mentioned no names, we are left to guess . . . but the East Riding population during the period of the investigations (1966-1969) did move from just below 250,000 to just above it.

Conclusion

In April 1972 the eleven plus examination was held for the last time for the majority of children in the East Riding. By September 1973 the transition to a fully comprehensive system was almost completed.

A number of modifications have been made to the scheme of reorganisation submitted by the Authority to D.E.S. in 1965. The East Riding will not have its Middle School. Market Weighton is to develop as a small comprehensive, retaining its children to the age of sixteen. This decision accords well with the wishes of the governors. The merger between Bridlington School and Bridlington High School for Girls has been called off, largely it would seem because of the unwillingness of the Bridlington School governors to surrender voluntary controlled status. The long feud between the Beverley Grammar School governors and the C.E.O. ended with the Chief Officer's retirement in March 1971. Since then events have moved very much in favour of those who have resisted attempts to alter the status and character of the grammar schools. Of overriding importance has been the policy and style of administration adopted by Mrs. Thatcher at the D.E.S. After the issue of Circular 10/70 she looked favourably upon local initiatives to preserve the grammar schools.[119]

Speaking at the N.U.T. Conference 1972, Mrs. Thatcher made clear the idea that a comprehensive school needed to be very large to be effective was no longer tenable. These attitudes have since been reiterated. [120] The new mood at the centre has provided governing bodies, especially those of aided schools, with strong backing to resist the pressures to reorganize.

Mrs. Thatcher's Circular 10/70 rallied the forces opposed to change and the new East Riding Chief Education Officer, John Bower, had a difficult and at times almost embarrassing task of attempting to implement policies which he inherited, as for example, when the contents of a letter from Lord Belstead, Parliamentary Under Secretary for Education and Science, to Patrick Wall, M.P., on the subject of Beverley reorganisation, was leaked to the press. [121] The letter caused quite a stir and gave a clear indication of the degree of sympathy with which the Department viewed the grammar school's case. Midway through 1973 confusion still persisted regarding the future pattern of secondary school organisation for Beverley and Bridlington. A decision from Mrs. Thatcher was expected before the Easter holidays but on 1st July this was still being awaited. The L.E.A. had no option but to inform parents that as the governors of the Beverley grammar school had made no proposal to change the school's character it must for the time being remain a selective school for boys. [122] Fifty-five boys were entered for selection to Beverley Grammar School in 1973. Only seven passed the test and entered the school. The governors still refused to change their minds about selection. However, on 18th March, 1974 with a hostile Labour government back in office and without the resources to go independent, they conceded defeat. [123] Bridlington School also suffered the embarrassment of a drastically reduced intake. This created overcrowding at Headlands School and pressure has mounted from the N.A.S. and N.U.T. in the Bridlington area for an end to selection and a return to the 1965/66 plan for secondary reorganisation. [124]

On 1st April, 1974 the East Riding County Council surrendered its powers to the new Humberside authority. The implications for educational administration were discussed by those opposed to the change in a report on the Local Government Bill: [125]

> there are not only two rural areas (East Riding and Lindsay) which, owing to geographical separation cannot be combined. There are also the two county boroughs, Hull and Grimsby, Scunthorpe (an excepted district) and Goole (a divisional executive). It will be a very long time before such a county can even remotely be regarded as having a unified educational system.

Reconciliation to the new order was made easier for some when it was announced that the East Riding C.E.O. had been appointed Director of Education for Humberside. Already new thinking is in evidence. Consultative committees, representing governing bodies, teachers and parents, are being set up to sound out local opinion and a detailed analysis of educational provision is being made to prepare the way for a development plan for Education in Humberside. [126]

NOTES

1. *Yorkshire Evening Press*, 8 Nov. 1943. At a morning session R. A. Butler met representatives of diocesan education committees. Conversations on educational reconstruction had been proceeding less formally for two years: *Hansard*, 16 July 1943 cols. 539-41.
2. East Riding of Yorkshire Education Committee Minutes 10 Jan. 1944 (henceforth cited as E.R.E.C. Minutes).
3. It has been suggested that the most important single factor in the successful administration of the schools by the local authorities after 1902 was the appointment of knowledgeable experts as their officials: P. H. J. H. Gosden, *Educational Administration in England and Wales* (1966), 189.
4. E.R.E.C. Minutes, 12 May 1944.
5. A favourite phrase of Victor Clark.
6. J. Lawson, *Endowed Grammar Schools of East Yorkshire* (1962), 30.
7. The C.E.O.'s valedictory speech quoted in *Hull Daily Mail*, 25 Jan. 1971.
8. There were two Part III authorities in the East Riding, Beverley and Bridlington. Both were too small to qualify for divisional executive status in 1944.
9. For the extent of Hadow reorganisation in the East Riding, see Appendix I.
10. Gosden, *op. cit.*, 181.
11. A. J. P. Taylor, *English History, 1914-45* (1965), 242.
12. *Cf.* M. Kogan and W. Van Der Eyken, *County Hall L.E.A.* (1973), 23-29.
13. The long-awaited volume on 'The History of Education in the Second World War', being written by Dr. P. H. J. H. Gosden, should clarify this.
14. Board of Education, *Report of the Consultative Committee on Secondary Education* (1938) xix-xxii, 291-92.
15. R. Pedley, *The Comprehensive School* (1963), 43.
16. *Hansard*, 29 July 1943, col. 1829.
17. R. Barker, *Education and Politics, 1900-1951* (1972), 84.
18. As prescribed by the Minister, Form 650.
19. T. W. Bamford, *The Evolution of Rural Education, 1850-1964* (1965), 63-69; V. Clark *The Condition of the Primary Schools in the East Riding of Yorkshire* (County Hall, 1967), 4-9.
20. Preamble to East Riding Development Plan, p.2.
21. Ministry of Education, *Circular 73* (1945).
22. Preamble, *op.cit.*, 3. In the early 1950s the East Riding began to develop its own farm institute on a 424 acre site at Bishop Burton.
23. The first *Report of the Joint Advisory Committee on Agricultural Education* (the Loveday Committee) (H.M.S.O., 1947), appears to have had some influence on the East Riding planners. See Appendix II (below).
24. It was envisaged that such a school might draw some of its pupils from other parts of the county, including perhaps some from urban areas who wanted to take up agricultural work. The school in fact evolved differently and without boarders.
25. Ministry of Education, *Circular 90* (1946).
26. *Ibid.*, para 6 (i)(a).
27. Berkshire Education Committee, *Development Plan*, p.14.
28. North Riding Education Committee, *Report by the Secretary on the modifications to the development plan for primary and secondary education proposed by the Minister of Education* (1947).
29. Ministry of Education, *Circular 144* (1947).
30. North Riding Education Committee, *op. cit.*, 2.
31. E.R.E.C. Minutes, 9 June 1947.
32. *The First Five Years, An account of the operation of the 1944 Act in the East Riding, 1945-50*, p.2.
33. *Ibid.*, p.41.
34. E.R.E.C. Minutes, 13 Dec. 1948. At this time about 20 Development Plans had been approved by the Minister. By the end of 1950, some 70 out of a total of 129.
35. E.R.E.C. Minutes, 6 June 1948.
36. Preamble, *op. cit.* 7.

37. J. A. G. Griffiths, *Central Departments and Local Authorities* (1966), 106.
38. E.R.E.C. Minutes, 20 Mar. 1946.
39. The Hut Operation for the Raising of the School Age programme comprised 6,838 teaching rooms, almost all of which were completed by the end of 1949. They were equipped with a special range of standardised utility furniture: *Education 1900-1950*, Cmnd. 8244, p.97.
40. T. W. Bamford, *op. cit.*, 79; *Rural Education, Aspects of Education No. 17, Journal of the Insitute of Education, University of Hull* (1973), 19-37.
41. *First Five Years, op. cit.*, 15-16.
42. Ministry of Education, *The Story of Post-War School Building* (1957).
43. E.R.E.C. Minutes, 23 Sept. 1946, Appendix 5 to Minute 197.
44. E.R.E.C. Minutes, 14 Dec. 1946, Appendix 4 to Minute 344.
45. E.R.E.C. Minutes, 14 Mar. 1946, Appendix 4 to Minute 436.
46. *Ibid.* The proposed distribution of capital expenditure could not be adhered to. Spending on secondary schools has exceeded the estimate but primary and special school has fallen behind. *Cf.* East Riding C.C., *Abstract of Accounts, 1969-70.*
47. Griffiths, *op. cit.*, 107.
48. Ministry of Education, *Pamphlet No. 33*, p.24.
49. E.R.E.C. Minutes, 27 Sept. 1948, Appendix 4 to Minute 199.
50. E.R.E.C. Minutes, 10 Jan. 1949.
51. *Ibid.*
52. *First Five Years, op cit.*, 55-56.
53. Ministry of Education, *Pamphlet No. 33*, p.3. Up to and including the 1949 programme L.E.A.s were not required to keep the cost of their projects within any prescribed limits.
54. *Ibid.*, p.26.
55. East Riding C.C., *Abstract of Accounts.* See Appendix III (below) for details.
56. Ministry of Education, *Pamphlet No. 33*, p.22.
57. *Ibid.*, Appendix II, p.69.
58. East Riding C.C., *Abstract of Accounts.* See Appendix III (below) for details.
59. E.R.E.C. Minutes, 7 Mar. 1949, Memorandum on Educational Building.
60. E.R.E.C. Minutes, 4 Feb. 1952, Memorandum to Ministry Circular 245.
61. D. Rubenstein and B. Simon, *The Evolution of the Comprehensive School* (1969), 88-89.
62. C.E.O., Memorandum, Policy for Secondary Education (October 1964), 16-17.
63. *Ibid.*, 16-17.
64. M. Kogan, *The Politics of Education* (1971), 20.
65. *Ibid.*, 50.
66. C.E.O., Memorandum, The Organisation of Secondary Education (1965).
67. At Hessle, South Hunsley, Willerby and South Holderness.
68. The D.E.S. calculated that a school of about 1,500 pupils would be able to develop a good sixth form.
69. The Organisation of Secondary Education, *op. cit.*, 11.
70. The Condition of Primary Schools, *op. cit.*, 20; Bamford, *op. cit.*, 51.
71. D.E.S., *Circular 10/65*, para. 39.
72. *The Public Schools Commission, First Report*, 1968, *Second Report*, 1970.
73. The Organisation of Secondary Education, *op. cit.*, 25.
74. *Ibid.*, 26.
75. Consultations with Governing Bodies and Teachers' Organisations: A Report by the C.E.O. (July 1966).
76. Cottingham and Bridlington (Headlands).
77. The C.E.O. was of the opinion that Market Weighton might be 'the one place in the East Riding where the educational interest might be best served by this type of organisation': Organisation of Secondary Education, *op. cit.*, 11.
78. Report of the Governors of the Beverley Grammar School on proposals put forward by the C.E.O. for the East Riding.
79. See above, p. 10.
80. Consultations with Governing Bodies, *op. cit.*, 18-32.

81. In the reorganisation of local government Filey became part of North Yorkshire.
82. C.E.O., Memorandum, The Observations of the D.E.S. on the Authority's Proposals for Reorganisation of Secondary Education (July 1967).
83. R. J. Buxton, *Local Government* (1970), 208-17.
84. C.E.O., Memorandum (July 1967), *op. cit.*
85. *Ibid.*, 2-3.
86. The all-age school was rapidly becoming extinct. One or two still survived in Hull and in the North and West Ridings.
87. E.R.E.C., Minutes, 30 Dec. 1957, Appendix 5 to Minute 147.
88. In 1948 it had been decided that special responsibility allowances, which at that time only applied to the grammar schools, should apply to all secondary schools: E.R.E.C., Minutes, 27 Sept. 1948.
89. *Cf.*, O. Banks, *Parity and Prestige in English Education* (1955), 219.
90. *Secondary Education for All. A New Drive*, Cmnd. 604 (1958).
91. E.R.E.C., Minutes, 22 Dec. 1958.
92. E.R.E.C., Minutes, 17 Mar. 1969.
93. Ministry of Education, *List 69* (1963).
94. Ministry of Education, *List 71* (1962).
95. B. E. Coates and R. M. Rawstron, *Regional Variations in Britain* (1970), 253.
96. *Ibid.*, 263-65.
97. *The Intermediate Areas*, (Report of a Committee under the Chairmanship of Sir Joseph Hunt), Cmnd. 3998 (1969).
98. *Ibid.*, 62.
99. Coates and Rawstron, *op. cit.*, 269-70.
100. G. Taylor and N. Ayres, *Born and Bred Unequal* (1969).
101. *Ibid.*, 3.
102. Rateable value 1969-70: £8,413,210; product of 1d. rate 1970: £34,106; population 1970: 252,830; R.V. per head of population: £33 5s. 7d.
103. Taylor and Ayres, *op. cit.*, 57.
104. Coates and Rawstron, *op. cit.*, 279.
105. Taylor and Ayres, *op. cit.*, 86-87.
106. The Condition of Primary Schools, *op. cit.*, 21-22.
107. D.E.S., *Statistics of Education, 1966*, Vol. 1.
108. Withernsea High School was awarded four posts of special responsibility in 1945-46—£100; £70; £65; £52: E.R.E.C., Minutes, 14 Mar. 1947. For the significance of the flexibility which existed until 1956 see P. H. J. H. Gosden, *The Evolution of a Profession* (1972), 72.
109. D.E.S., Survey of Courses for Teachers sponsored by the L.E.A. of the East Riding of Yorkshire, January 1962 to December 1964 (Misc. 14/64).
110. E.g., Sir Martin Roseveare, Sir John Maud, Sir Fred Clarke, Sir James Scott Watson, Sir Christopher Cox, Sir Charles Morris, Dr. Marjorie Reeves, Rodger Armfelt, Henry Morris and S. H. Wood.
111. E.g., the Leeds Labour group were able to hold up the introduction of the G.C.E into secondary modern schools: Kogan and Van der Eyken, *op. cit.*, 171.
112. See above, pp. 11-24
113. See above, pp. 13-14
114. Coates and Rawstron, *op. cit.*, 279.
115. Taylor and Ayres, *op. cit.*, 82.
116. *Education*, 9 Mar. 1973, p.304.
117. *Ibid.*, 23 and 30 Mar., 13 Apr. 1973.
118. *Enquiry into efficiency of L.E.A.s, Royal Commission on Local Government, 1966-1969* Vol. 3, Appendix II.
119. D.E.S., *Circular 10/70, The Organisation of Secondary Education.*
120. *Guardian*, 13 Mar. 1973.
121. *Hull Daily Mail*, 5 Jan. 1971.
122. C.E.O., letter to parents of boys in their final year of primary education in the Beverley area (April 1973).

123. *Hull Daily Mail*, 19 Mar. 1974.
124. *Bridlington Free Press*, 4 Apr. 1974.
125. East Riding C.C., *Report on Local Government Reorganisation* (1971), 3.
126. *Hull Daily Mail*, 12 July 1974.

APPENDIX I

Hadow Reorganisation in the East Riding

There had been some reorganisation of elementary schools into departments, i.e. all-age schools with Senior Divisions. Board of Education, *List 49* (1938) indicates how far this had developed.

East Riding (excluding Bridlington and Beverley):

> 1,547 pupils over 11 in reorganized departments.
> 4,430 pupils over 11 in unreorganized departments.

Beverley:

> 286 of the 677 pupils in reorganized departments.

Bridlington:

> All 738 pupils over 11 in reorganized departments. The majority were in the two senior schools which opened 1935 (boys) and 1938 (girls).

The Beverley performance was a poor one. Two points can be made in its favour however. First, there were authorities with an even worse record: e.g., Hyde, Chelmsford, and Newport (I.o.W.) where there had been no reorganization at all. Secondly, the Beverley authority had made a modest start towards providing a senior elementary school. In 1937 it purchased a 9·48 acre site at St. Giles Croft.

The East Riding progress as a whole was not impressive when contrasted with:

North Riding:

> 6,773 pupils in reorganized departments.
> 5,835 pupils in unreorganized departments.

Northumberland

> 7,649 pupils in reorganized departments.
> 8,496 pupils in unreorganized departments.

APPENDIX II

Extracts from the Loveday Committee Report, 1945

The Joint Advisory Committee on Agricultural Education had been asked by the Minister of Education 'to give immediate consideration to the question whether courses designed to prepare boys and girls for work on the land or in rural industries should be provided with technical schools in rural areas, and, if so, what should be the nature and content of such courses'. The information was urgently required because L.E.A.s had to prepare and submit development plans before 1 April 1946.

The Committee was of the opinion that a more advanced course of training similar in character but differing in depth and scope, could and should be provided, as an alternative to the academic education of the grammar school, for abler boys and girls of a practical bent who would in future hold responsible posts in the industry. It recommended that a pre-agricultural course should be a three-year course for pupils from 13 to 16.

The Committee discussed the advantages and disadvantages for pre-agricultural courses in the following types of school:

1. **The Agricultural Technical School,** i.e. the counterpart of the junior technicals in the towns. The Committee felt that there was a danger that such a school 'may easily degenerate into a trade school of the narrowest kind'.

2. **The Rural Junior Polytechnic.** No such school (i.e. one which provided pre-vocational courses alongside an agricultural course) then existed.

3. **The addition of an agricultural side to an urban technical school.** This was possible 'where a rural area abuts a town of moderate size which possesses a technical school'.

4. **An agricultural side in a rural grammar school.** Such a course, the Committee felt, would acquire ready-made advantages of grammar school prestige.

5. **The Multilateral School.** It would need to be 5-form entry and a school of that size with three sides would probably be found unwieldy.

6. **Pre-agricultural and allied courses in chosen modern schools.** The Committee felt that in some rural areas the most convenient arrangement might be to provide pre-vocational courses of technical school standard in chosen modern schools. Residential accommodation on a larger scale would be required and possibly additional land.

7. **Pre-agricultural courses for the 'A' stream in rural modern schools.** Possibilities 1 to 6 were all 'selective' schools.

APPENDIX III

The Evolution of the East Riding Secondary School Building Programme

School Areas	All-age Elementary Schools		Development Plan Proposals for Secondary Schools, 1948					Type of School Provided and Date
	To be Discontinued	To become Primary Schools	Existing Grant-Aided Schools to be used by the L.E.A.	Proposed New Secondary Schools	Proposed Date for Building	Size in Forms	Loan Sanction £	
Barlby	8	5	Selby Grammar, Drax Grammar, Goole Grammar	1 Modern/Technical (A)	1952-3	3	172,746 1957-58	1960 (A)
Beverley	10	4	Beverley Grammar (Boys), Beverley High School (Girls)	1 Modern/Technical (A) (Commercial)	1947-8	4	(Erection) 275,250 1948 (Site) 11,162 1947	1950 (A)
				1 Modern/Technical (B) (Rural)	Post 1953	4		
Bridlington	9	0	Bridlington School (Boys), Bridlington High School (Girls), Bridlington St. George's (Senior Elementary)	1 Modern/Technical (A) (Boys)	Post 1953	4	(Site) 42,479 1959-62 (Erection) 294,618 1962-67	1965 (A) (Mixed)
Brough	6	0		1 Modern/Technical (A) (Grammar School Pupils to Hessle)	1951-52	3	(Erection) 140,176 1954 (Extensions) 1965	1956 (A)
Cottingham (Haltemprice)	2	2	Beverley Grammar School (Boys), Beverley High School (Girls), Hull Maintained Secondary Schools, Hymers College	1 Modern/Technical (A)	1948-49	4	(Site) 7,670 1947 (Erection) 188,913 1951-58	1955 (A)

35

Development Plan Proposals for Secondary Schools, 1948

School Areas	All-age Elementary Schools		Existing Grant-Aided Schools to be used by the L.E.A.	Proposed New Secondary Schools	Proposed Date for Building	Size in Forms	Loan Sanction £	Type of School Provided and Date
	To be Discontinued	To become Primary Schools						
Driffield	10	0		1 Modern/Technical (A) 1 Grammar (B) or 1 Grammar/Mod./Tech. (C) (Combined Secondary)	1948-9 1948-9 after 1953	4/5 2 6/7	(Site) 9,152 1949-55 (Erection) 155,930 149,536 1953-55	1955 (A)
Filey	10	3	Bridlington School (Boys) Bridlington High School (Girls)	1 Modern/Technical (A)	After 1953	3/4	(Site) 4.165 1957-59 (Erection) 166,879 1959	1961 (A)
Fulford	7	3	York Maintained Schools York Bar Convent York College for Girls York St. Peter's School	1 Modern/Technical (A)	After 1953	3	(Site) 4,055 1960-61 (Erection) 204,055	1963 (A)
Hessle (Haltemprice)	0	1	Hull Maintained Schools Hymers College	1 Modern/Technical (Boys) 1 Modern/Technical (Girls) 1 Grammar School (C)	1950-51 1950-51 After 1953	3 3 2/3	Tranby House (Extensions) 36,391 1950-56 159,382 1963-67	1950 (A) (Mixed)

Development Plan Proposals for Secondary Schools, 1948

School Areas	All-age Elementary Schools		Existing Grant-Aided Schools to be used by the L.E.A.	Proposed New Secondary Schools	Proposed Date for Building	Size in Forms	Loan Sanction £	Type of School Provided and Date
	To be Discontinued	To become Primary Schools						
Hedon-Preston	8	3	Hull Maintained Schools Hymers College	1 Modern/Technical (A)	1952-53	3/4	(Erection) 365,698 1950 255,835 1969	1954 (A)
Hornsea	11	7	Bridlington School (Boys) Bridlington High School (Girls) Beverley Grammar (Boys) Beverley High School (Girls)	1 Modern/Technical (A)	1949-50	4	(Site) 8,293 1953-55 (Erection) 154,336 1955-56	1958 (A)
Howden	9	3	Goole Grammar	1 Modern/Technical (A)	After 1953	3	(Erection) 178,410 1960	1963 (A)
Market Weighton	7	2	Beverley Grammar (Boys) Beverley High School (Girls) Pocklington School	1 Modern (A)	1947-48	2	(Erection) 184,500 1950-58	1952 (A)
Norton	8	4	Malton Grammar	1 Modern/Technical (A)	1949-50	3	(Site) 3,613 1959 (Erection) 174,252 1960	1963 (A)

Development Plan Proposals for Secondary Schools, 1948

School Areas	All-age Elementary Schools		Existing Grant-Aided Schools to be used by the L.E.A.	Proposed New Secondary Schools	Proposed Date for Building	Size in Forms	Loan Sanction £	Type of School Provided and Date
	To be Discontinued	To become Primary Schools						
Pocklington	17	2	Pocklington School York Maintained Schools York Bar Convent York College for Girls York St. Peter's	1 Modern (A)	After 1953	3	(Erection) 186.411 1956-61	1958 (A)
Sledmere	5	4		1 Modern (Grammar School Pupils to Driffield) (A)	After 1953	2		No provision; children attend Driffield Secondary School
Willerby (Haltemprice)	0	3	Hull Maintained Schools Hull Hymers College	1 Modern/Technical (A)	After 1953	5	(Erection) 153.475 1957 351.285 1966-68	1959 (A)
Withernsea	8	3	Withernsea County Secondary	1 Combined Secondary	1951-52	5	(Erection) 294.500 1950-58	1955 (A)

38

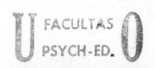

MAP 1

EAST RIDING ELEMENTARY
SCHOOLS WITH PUPILS
AGED 11-14 IN 1945

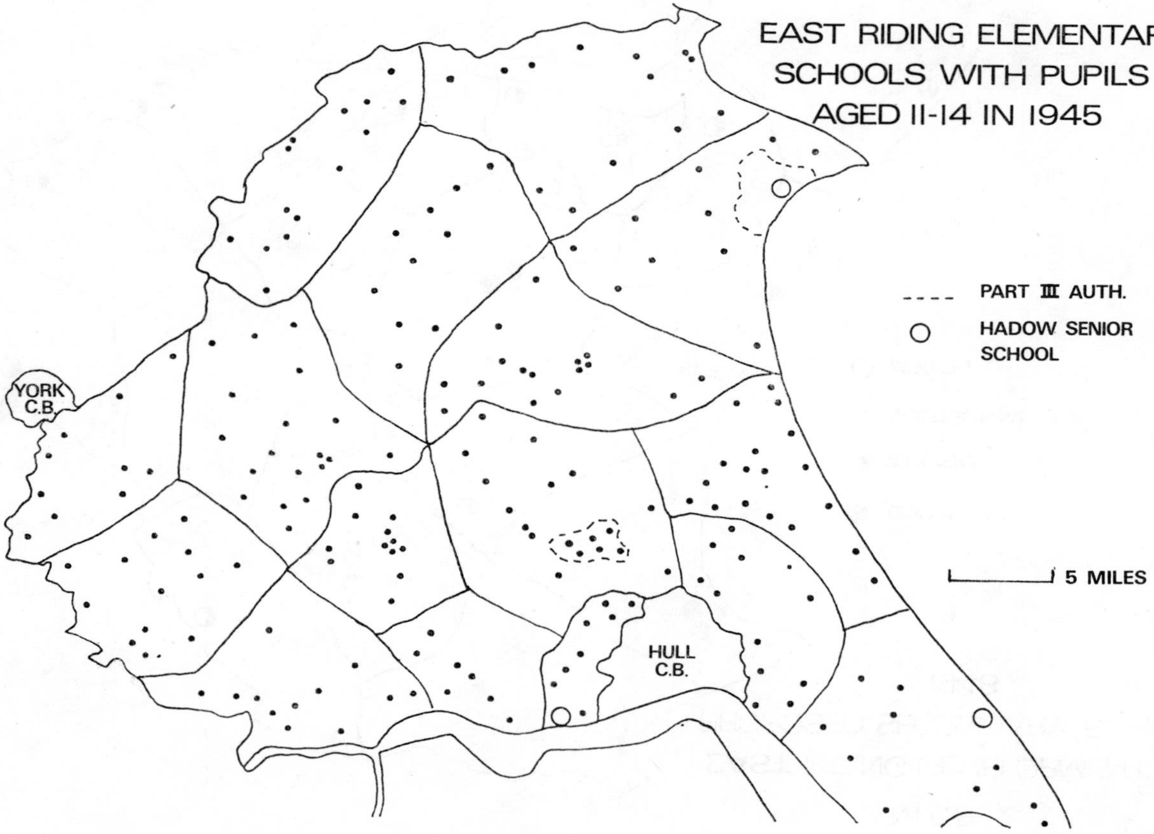

PART III AUTH. ----

HADOW SENIOR ○
SCHOOL

5 MILES

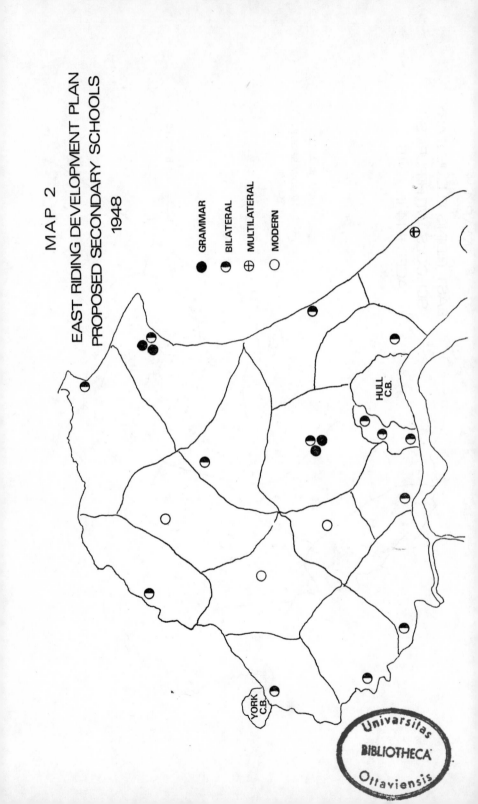

MAP 2
EAST RIDING DEVELOPMENT PLAN
PROPOSED SECONDARY SCHOOLS
1948

● GRAMMAR
◐ BILATERAL
⊕ MULTILATERAL
○ MODERN

HULL
C.B.

YORK
C.B.